Six Minutes with God

Six Minutes with God

A 90-DAY DEVOTIONAL WITH THE GOD WHO SPEAKS

JULIE WALL

Harp & Sword
MEDIA

Published by Harp & Sword Media LLC
129 S. Main St., #260
Grapevine, TX 76051
www.harpandswordmedia.com

Cover design by Joe DeLeon of DeLeon Design

ISBN (paperback): 979-8-99973-943-8
ISBN (ebook): 979-8-99973-944-5

10 9 8 7 6 5 4 3 2 1

Printed in the United States of America

This book is dedicated to my children, my arrows:
Stella, Kingston, and Kenway.
May you heed God's voice all your days
and, in doing so, find your own.
May my ceiling be your floor.

*"Like arrows in the hands of a warrior
are children born in one's youth."*
Psalm 127:4

Contents

Acknowledgments

A special thanks to Eric Freesmeier, "Poppie," for being the first to read my full manuscript and enthusiastically copyedit, advise, and encourage.

Thank you, Debbie Freesmeier, "WoWo," for leading me to accept Jesus in your minivan as a little girl and continually fanning the flame. Without you, this wouldn't be.

Thank you, Mom, for your unconditional love and support and for always being a bright light when my world seemed gray. Your endless joy inspires me daily.

To my army of prayer warriors, my amazing family and friends, and everyone who said, "Do it," and believed that I could, taking that faith to the throne room on my behalf, I am eternally grateful.

Introduction

Speak, Lord, for your servant is listening.
1 Samuel 3:9

Have you ever had a conversation with someone who was such a talker that you couldn't get a word in edgewise? If you have, you know how frustrating it can feel, as you sit there, hoping the person will pause and take a breath so you can get a word in, offer feedback, or even just share what's on your mind. You're left feeling as though the person might as well have spoken to a brick wall, if all they wanted to do was hear themselves talk.

Now, consider your own prayer time with God.

Are you the one dominating the conversation?

If God were physically sitting on your couch with you during your quiet time, could you even imagine talking the whole time when you have the God of the universe right there able to speak to you? The audacity. But the truth is, for many of us dear sheep of God's flock, the majority of us are guilty of this.

What is prayer to you?

Does prayer resemble a venting session or checking off a wish list of requests? It is an incredible privilege that God made it possible for us to talk to Him by the power of the indwelling of the Holy Spirit. It is literally a miraculous lifeline! When we speak, God listens and acts. However, prayer is intended to be a *conversation*.

God loves to hear from us and definitely wants us to talk to Him. But He wants us to hear from Him too. And yes, we do hear from God through the Bible, His Word, which is incredible, infallible, alive, and powerful (Hebrews 4:12), and never to be discounted. But God also wants to speak to us about our own personal day-to-day stuff.

I think of God's Word being evergreen because it is universally true and applies to all people, in any circumstance, any day, in any age. But what about when your questions and needs are a bit more specific? "Do I take this job, Lord?" "God, how do I love my rebellious teen through this season?" "How should I respond to this difficult person, Lord?" "Do I really want, or 'need,' fries with that?" God's got this covered too. Jesus sent the Holy Spirit to be with His people when He was leaving the earth and said:

> But I tell you the truth, it is for your advantage that I go away; for if I do not go away, the Helper (Comforter, Advocate, Intercessor—Counselor, Strengthener, Standby) will not come to you; but if I go, I will send Him (the Holy Spirit) to you [to be in close fellowship with you].
>
> —John 16:7, AMP

It is mind-blowing that Jesus said it was actually better that He leave us so the Holy Spirit could come to us. What is better than Jesus in the flesh? But God is Three in One, and the Holy Spirit is just as much God as God the Father and Jesus the Son! And via the Holy Spirit, God is able to be with all of us, at all times, anywhere, Wi-Fi or not. Legit.

The Holy Spirit is called our Intercessor, so yes, when we pray, He intercedes for us on behalf of our prayers, but He is also called our Counselor. Well, counselors are great listeners, but if I paid to go to a counselor who only listened to me talk and never gave me feedback or advice, I'd feel shortchanged.

But the Holy Spirit is the perfect Counselor. God is talking, but we may not be listening. Think about it: What is the point of talking to God about our troubles if we aren't going to stop and listen for His feedback, of asking Him what to do and then walking away before giving Him a chance to answer us?

Hence the point of this book.

A few years back God began to deal with me in this very area. Filled with the Holy Spirit, I knew God had a way of speaking to me through His Word and even interrupting my thoughts when I was not actively taking time to listen, because He loves me that dearly. But I felt I was shortchanging God during my prayer times, mostly listening to myself talk about what I thought and felt, begging God to fix things, but then not asking Him what He thought, how He felt about my situation, or how I should partner with Him to do His will. So I set out to discipline myself to end every prayer time by giving God the floor, closing my trap, and letting Him speak. And if you're like me—and most of you are, if you are honest—you have a short attention span. But I decided I wouldn't let that stop me. That's why this book is called *Six Minutes with God*, not sixty.

Sometimes we overshoot.

Have you ever decided you're going to start a stringent diet and exercise plan? You've lived on fast food and haven't worked out in years, but you decide to get healthy. However, instead of baby steps, you say you're going to exercise for an hour every day and have no sweets, no sugar, and only healthy food twenty-four seven. How long did that plan last? My bet is not long. And oftentimes, instead of just scaling back when we overshoot, we get frustrated with our failings and just quit altogether.

The same can happen with spiritual disciplines. We tell ourselves, "I am going to go sit in my closet and listen to God for an hour every day." But that's such a tall order for our fleshly selves that we don't follow through. We give up quickly and, instead of doing something, end up doing nothing at all. When I set out on my journey to cultivate a prayer life that was more of a conversation than a voicemail message, I felt God reminding me not to get bound up in legalistic expectations. Baby steps were not only OK but honorable in His eyes. And trust me, disciplining ourselves to listen for God to speak is harder than it sounds. That's how I ended up with a plan to listen to God for six minutes. I actually started by telling myself, "God is OK with me starting small, so I will set a timer for five minutes to listen to Him."

But after realizing it took at least a minute for me to even really get my mind quiet, I added another minute so I wasn't taking more of the mere five minutes a day when I was trying to empty my brain space of my own all-important thoughts (sarcasm intended) so that the God of the universe could talk to me for the intended five minutes. That's what this book is about.

I'm going to invite you to the challenge of cultivating the discipline of spending time every day quieting your mind and listening to God for at least six minutes. And I'm going to share what God shared with me during my precious "God times" for inspiration and prompting. It's kind of like looking at someone else's notes, because it can help to see what it looks like when someone else is already doing something you want to do. You'll see some of my words from God are longer and some are very short, maybe just a sentence or two. That's just how it goes, and you'll probably find the same to be true for you. Sometimes I hear only a brief word from God, maybe because that's all He had to say, or maybe my listening was less than ideal that day; I'm not sure which, but that's OK too.

Why a timer or time limit?

You may find it weird that I set a timer or that there is a time limit in this discipline practice at all. That in itself seems a little legalistic, or like how dare I give God only six minutes? Let me be clear: The timer is definitely not for God; it is for me. The God I serve is not bound by time, or a timer, for that matter, and I surely never want to confine Him. But as I'm guessing it is with many other people, we have many of what a preacher I love calls "weapons of mass distractions" (Jeff Perry, St. Louis Family Church) and many responsibilities vying for our attention all day long: workdays to start, kids to feed and drive around, and appointments to make.

The reason I set a timer is so I can tell myself: "Julie, there is nothing that will need your immediate attention for the next six minutes. The timer will alert you when six minutes has passed. This way you aren't wondering how much time is left while you are trying to let God occupy your thoughts." This is the point of the timer. Often, God is not done in six minutes, so I do not cut Him off. Maybe you'll want to try this your own way and change things up a bit. That's OK too! I encourage you to discuss that with God. After all, He knows you and all your little quirks best, and He would love to help you figure out a method that works best for you. For me, He knows I am type A, so this is where I've landed because the structure helps me.

So here we are. Hopefully six minutes is a starting point, and you can grow in the discipline of listening to God longer, not just in your quiet time but through cultivating the ability and habit of listening for His still, small voice throughout the day. *(Note: That became another issue God eventually addressed with me. He told me not to leave Him on the couch, where I would have my quiet time, because He wanted to join me in the rest of my day too!)* My prayer is that if you haven't cultivated a habit of hearing from God but desire to, this book will inspire you to discipline yourself in this habit because He loves you and He would love to speak to your heart.

How Do You Hear
from God Anyway?

Whether you turn to the right or to the left,
your ears will hear a voice behind you, saying,
"This is the way; walk in it."
Isaiah 30:21

"This whole 'hearing from God' concept is totally foreign to me."

If you picked up this book and are thinking that, I am so glad you are here! Do not feel bad, discouraged, or totally weirded out. Hearing from God is possible, but it is a discipline that takes practice. In fact, the key verse I shared at the beginning of the introduction is from a time when Samuel, who was a priest, then a prophet, and an incredibly significant person in the Bible, also had to learn this discipline. First Samuel 3 is an awesome chapter and one I find quite comical. When Samuel was a young boy, he served the Lord under the leadership and training of Eli. In this chapter God called out to Samuel for the first time while he was sleeping. Samuel kept thinking Eli was calling him, and after he bothered Eli three times, Eli assured Samuel that he was not talking to him and told him to go back to bed. Finally, Eli realized it was God calling Samuel, but Samuel didn't recognize the voice of God yet. So Eli instructed Samuel, "Go and lie down, and if he calls you, say, 'Speak, Lord, for your servant is listening'" (1 Samuel 3:9). Samuel did just that, and he did in fact hear from God. From then on, Samuel became well acquainted with God's voice and heard from Him often throughout the rest of his life.

OK, but that was Samuel.

Maybe you think only special people hear from God, or that it was just an Old Testament thing. But Jesus said in John 10:27 (ESV): "My sheep hear My voice, and I know them, and they follow me." In this analogy Jesus referred to Himself as a shepherd, so sheep are simply followers of Jesus. If you have not made Jesus your Lord and Savior and made the decision to follow Him, you can pause and do so right now. Please look at the back of this book for more information about receiving Jesus, and join us back here after you have made that awesome decision. If you have, that's right, *baaaa*. Guess what, you're a sheep. And it doesn't matter if you're a preacher sheep, a teacher sheep, a lunch lady sheep, a construction worker sheep, a servant sheep, an old sheep, or a young sheep—you're still a sheep, and God is your Shepherd. God speaks and guides us, and He has given us the ability to hear Him.

Fine. *Baaaa.* But really, how?

Most of the time, people do not hear God speaking to them audibly, as Samuel did. I have never had this happen to me either, but when we talk about hearing from God, it is really God speaking to your heart, bringing something to your mind, or leaving an impression on your thoughts. As with getting to know someone, it takes developing a relationship and growing in familiarity until you can recognize that person's voice apart from all others. The same is true with God. The best way to get to know God is to study His Word, the Bible, which reveals His character, and what He says is true and good versus what He says is false and bad. Jesus also said of His sheep that they will follow Him and not a stranger's voice because they will know the difference and not be deceived (John 10:4–5).

We get to know God's voice and character and what aligns with the will of God by studying the words of the Bible. In fact, the Bible should be the standard-bearer that we hold all other words up against. That's why it is so important to study and know the Word, because if we think or believe anything that goes against His written Word, we know it is not from God. Second Corinthians 10:5 says that we are to "demolish arguments and every pretension that sets itself up against the knowledge of God, and we take captive every thought to make it obedient to Christ." As we are listening for God's voice and writing down what He says to us, we should always ensure these words align with His Word. In fact, God often brings a Bible verse to my mind as I am listening to Him. It is super cool how He will bring up a verse I haven't thought of in a long while, and I will know it is Him speaking to me, recalling to my mind something He wants me to remember. It really is an incredible experience to learn to hear God for yourself, so let's get to it! The final way to learn to hear from God is simply practicing. Put away distractions, quiet your mind, and say, "Speak, Lord, for your servant is listening." Let's do this.

A Prayer for the Reader
of These Pages

Father God, I lift before You the person who's holding this book. I know it pleases You that they have a desire to grow in their relationship with You by leaning in and posturing themselves to hear what You want to say. Lord, Your Word teaches us that You withhold no good thing from those who walk uprightly, and greater intimacy with You is a very good thing! I ask, therefore, boldly with faith, in partnership with the reader of this prayer, that You would give them the grace to hear Your words for them. I thank You, Father God, that You will open their spiritual ears to hear. May the words of Isaiah 50:4–5 become their testimony, and morning by morning may You awaken them to hear as those being taught, and as You open their ears, may they turn to hear Your perfect instruction. It's in Jesus' mighty name I pray, amen. (See Psalm 84:11, Mark 11:24, and Isaiah 50:4–5.)

Disclaimer

As I stated in the introduction, the supreme Word of God, the Bible, is the true, infallible authority for believers in Christ. As you read what I have heard God speak to me, please know that this vessel is not perfect. My utmost hope and desire is to honor God with everything I write down for you within the pages of this book. But please, even with what I share, put what you have been taught into practice and weigh everything you hear—my words or anyone else's, for that matter—up against the Word of God, the Bible.

Rejoice always, pray continually, give thanks in all circumstances; for this is God's will for you in Christ Jesus. Do not quench the Spirit. Do not treat prophecies with contempt but test them all; hold on to what is good, reject every kind of evil.

1 Thessalonians 5:16–22

Day 1

A Word from God on

Living Life to the Fullest

I love you, and I am proud of you. I am with you; have *fun* today. Shine *bright* for me. I know you can, and I love to see you shine. You are my child and deserve the best (not because of what you've done but because of what Jesus did for you), but be willing to hand that off to the least among you, remembering that I am your source, your constant, your Father, your strong support. I will never leave you or forsake you. This life together is an adventure; savor it. Don't settle in any area.

Don't worry about tomorrow, for each day has enough of its own stuff to think about. Don't get ahead of Me, and don't allow pride to rule you, thinking you have to accomplish *all* right now. We'll do it together, one thing at a time.

Be led by wisdom, self-control, and self-restraint.

The devil rushes; I am patient, so in that regard, be like Me.

I love you!

Time to adventure together.

> But seek first his kingdom and his righteousness, and all these things will be given to you as well. Therefore do not worry about tomorrow, for tomorrow will worry about itself. Each day has enough trouble of its own.
> —Matthew 6:33–34

God, what do You have to say to me about how I am living my life?

Day 2

Submitting to God's Timing

Focus on what I place in front of you. Bring Me into the details of your day. Let's do life together. Patience and self-control are powerful assets. You are left exposed and open a door to the enemy when you forsake self-control.

Like a city whose walls are broken through is a person who lacks self-control.

—Proverbs 25:28

God, are there areas I have gotten ahead of You, or do I need to get moving? What is one area of my life where I can work on exercising greater self-control?

Day 3

Planning Versus Worrying

Don't worry about tomorrow. Plan, but don't worry, and know the difference. Worry doesn't include the "God" factor, for all things are possible to him who believes.

If I can? Don't worry, I can, 100 percent!

> Not by might, nor by power, but by my Spirit, says the LORD of hosts.
> —Zechariah 4:6, ESV

God, what areas of my life do I need to quit worrying about?

Day 4

A Word from God on

Praying for the Desires of Your Heart

It is coming. I've got this, and I've got you. You are my child, and I want the best for you. Good things are worth the wait. Rest in Me. I know best, so rest.

> Be still before the LORD [and rest] and wait patiently for him [trust Him].
> —Psalm 37:7, ESV

God, what do You think about the desires of my heart? Are they in line with Your desires for me?

Day 5

Parenting and Other Overwhelming Duties

Are you modeling love, patience, and peace, or anxiety and hurried-ness? Do you show an uncaring attitude toward what concerns them? You might think you are teaching others strength, but not caring is not strength. You can encourage them and reinforce proper behavior while showing care and empathy too. I can help you strike a balance.

If I speak in all the languages of the earth and of angels, but didn't love others, I would only be a noisy gong or a clanging symbol.

—1 Corinthians 13:1, NLT

*God, whom can I display more love to by simply slowing down and car-
ing more? What are some practical ways I can do this starting today?*

Day 6

A Word from God on

Keeping Him First

Keep Me first, no matter what, and in this way you will always remain on the right path I have for you. I love you! I am proud of you, and I am excited for your today *and* your future. *Both* are exciting, child. Stay excited. Let's enjoy this day together.

> He leads me in paths of righteousness for His name's sake.
> —Psalm 23:3, ESV

God, is there anywhere I have veered off the course You have for me?

Day 7

Trusting in What We Cannot See

I love you. Stay on task. You've got this. I'm proud of you. I am helping you and will continue to help you. I am making divine connections. Often the boss is working behind closed doors for the benefit of all, but it may not be time to share the vision with His team. Continue to trust Me.

> It is God who works in you, both to will and to work for his good pleasure.
> —Philippians 2:13, ESV

What is it You are telling me to keep doing my part in, trusting that You'll also do Your part?

Day 8

Weakness

My power is made perfect in your weakness, when you recognize your total dependence on Me, because then I can do above and beyond for you, more than what you are capable of yourself.

> But he said to me, "My grace is sufficient for you, for my power is made perfect in weakness." Therefore I will boast all the more gladly in my weaknesses, so that the power of Christ may rest upon me. For the sake of Christ, then, I am content with weaknesses, insults, hardships, persecutions, and calamities. For when I am weak, then I am strong.
>
> —2 Corinthians 12:9–10, ESV

God, is there an area I am still stubbornly trying to manage in my own strength that I need to give up to You?

Day 9

A Word from God on

Distractions

Get your eyes back on Me. Die to your flesh; it depreciates, but the Spirit appreciates. In Me you have life, liberty, and peace. That's what I have and what I want for you. Don't settle. Stick close to Me. Invite Me into all things because I won't force My way in, but I make all things better and heal all situations. May I join you today?

> I keep my eyes always on the LORD. With him at my right hand, I will not be shaken. Therefore my heart is glad and my tongue rejoices; my body also will rest secure, because you will not abandon me to the realm of the dead, nor will you let your faithful one see decay. You make known to me the path of life; you will fill me with joy in your presence, with eternal pleasures at your right hand.
>
> —Psalm 16:8–11

Are there ways I have taken my eyes off You, God, settling for less than Your best?

Day 10

Mercy for Myself and Others

Show mercy as I have shown you mercy. Don't go about as someone without help, who doesn't know any better. In Me you have all that you need (and the ability to do all that I'm asking you to do). Rejoice! Be glad! I have redeemed you, and I call you Mine. Do not give the devil a foothold by falling for his schemes (and seeking revenge). Keep the peace, walk in joy, laugh, enjoy the present, and relax in Me. I will strengthen you.

> Don't be afraid, for I am with you. Don't be discouraged, for I am your God. I will strengthen you and help you. I will hold you up with my victorious right hand.
>
> —Isaiah 41:10, NLT

God, remind me of how You have shown me mercy and where I need to extend more of the same.

Day 11

A Word from God on

Pride and Humility

The humble receive My favor, so in cases where they are wrongly judged or misunderstood, they do not need to strive to defend themselves. But you must first be brought low and not think too highly of yourself. Some actions result from a seed of pride. Just as you don't like being misjudged, don't jump to conclusions about others. Pride leads to self-defense; humility, instead, relies on My defense, which is best.

Humble yourselves, therefore, under the mighty hand of God so that at the proper time He may exalt you.

—1 Peter 5:6, ESV

God, in what situations, or with whom, do I need to humble myself?

Day 12

A Word from God on

Good Days and Bad Days

Behold, I am with you always, even to the end of the age. In the good places and the bad, on good days and bad, I am right there, but you're far better off if you acknowledge My presence and invite Me into your moments. When things go well, it's easy to give Me praise, but you need Me even more when things are tough. In those moments, stop and meet with Me. There is never too little time to do that. I hold time. If I have to stop the sun for you, I will, but most likely that's not necessary. You just need to slow down. Be still, and know that I am God.

Then Joshua spoke to the LORD in the day when the LORD delivered up the Amorites before the children of Israel, and he said in the sight of Israel: "Sun, stand still over Gibeon, and Moon, in the valley of Aijalon." So the sun stood still, and the moon stopped, til the people had revenge upon their enemies. Is this not written in the Book of Jashar? So the sun stood still in the midst of heaven, and did not hasten to go down for about a whole day. And there has been no day like that, before it or after it, that the LORD heeded the voice of a man; for the LORD fought for Israel.

—Joshua 10:12–14, NKJV

God, in what ways can I practice actively inviting You into my daily life, good or bad?

Day 13

A Word from God on

Surrendering

Do right, and live. No secrets. Die to the flesh. Die to reasoning and excuse making. Decide now to do Me good, not harm, and don't mar My image in the earth all the days of your life. My hand of blessing will remain on you. I have been patient with you when you hesitated, but you know what you need to do. I will strengthen you. Don't settle for less than My best for you because My best is *best*! Trust Me, it is coming for you. Let go of the less than so you can take hold of the best.

> But one thing I do: Forgetting what is behind and straining toward what is ahead, I press on toward the goal to win the prize for which God has called me heavenward in Christ Jesus.
>
> —Philippians 3:13–14

> She brings him good, not harm, all the days of her life.
>
> —Proverbs 31:12

God, are there areas I need to bring into submission to You?

Day 14

A Word from God on

Casting Your Cares

Be sure to rest; I will take care of you. *Enjoy* this day. Be intentional in your interactions: quick to listen, slow to speak. Slow down. Pause and breathe when you feel anxiety rise, and ask Me to help put things back into proper perspective. Cast all your cares upon Me, for I care for you. I care more about you than the cares themselves. In the same way, care more about people than the things involved in your relationship with them. People matter more than the stuff or the cares.

> Cast all your anxiety on him because he cares for you.
>
> —1 Peter 5:7

God, reveal Your perspective on complicated situations and relation-ships, and show me how I can work on loving Your people more rather than caring about the stuff associated with them.

Day 15

A Word from God on

The People in Your Life

Everyone in your life is there for a reason. Everyone. Even if just for a brief passing through. See them differently.

> Do not be interested only in your own life, but be interested in the lives of others.
>
> —Philippians 2:4, NCV

God, how can I intentionally display the love of Jesus more so to those who pass through my life?

Day 16

A Word from God on

Speaking Life

Watch for opportunities to be a blessing and speak encouragement to people today. One word can change a person's entire trajectory. Words are powerful, so don't take them lightly. Be slow to speak and quick to listen, as sometimes listening is the most powerful display of love you can show.

> Let every person be quick to hear, slow to speak, slow to anger. . . . If anyone thinks he is religious and does not bridle his tongue but deceives his heart, this person's religion is worthless.
>
> —James 1:19, 26, ESV

God, in what ways do I need to bridle my tongue and close my mouth, and in what ways do I need to speak up and speak life?

Day 17

A Word from God on

Doing and Handling All the Things

You are not Me and can't do it all, but you can do all things I ask of you through Christ who strengthens you. Lean on Me for guidance, and take a time-out with Me when you feel the stress rising. Let Me filter the situation so you can see it with a spiritual and eternal perspective. This way with My help you can respond appropriately.

I can do all things through Christ who strengthens me.
—Philippians 4:13, NKJV

Your Six Minutes:
What Is God Saying to You Today?

God, from Your point of view, in which areas of my life do I need a renewed perspective?

Day 18

A Word from God on

Authority

Intentionally take ground for the kingdom of God. Be an atmosphere changer. Invite Me into every interaction you encounter, and trust Me to lead your words by actively inviting Me into your thoughts. Pause and ask Me, "Lord, what are You saying about this?" instead of focusing on what you want or think.

> I will give you the keys of the kingdom of heaven; whatever you bind on earth will be bound in heaven, and whatever you loose on earth will be loosed in heaven.
>
> —Matthew 16:19

God, in what ways am I relinquishing the authority that You've given me to be a world changer for You? What is one proactive change I can make to be alert and take more ground with intentionality?

A Word from God on

Walking in Love

Love My people—*all* of them. See people through *My* lens.

We love because he first loved us.

—1 John 4:19

What Is God Saying to You Today?

God, is there someone whom I have a hard time loving or lack grace for? Show me Your love for them, and give me insight from Your perfect perspective so that I may love them well.

Day 20

A Word from God on

Surrendering Control

Trust Me and let go. I abide where reasoning ends: in faith. I don't require you to know all the answers because that's My job. And I won't let you down or abandon you. Step forward with confidence, by faith.

> The Lord is my strength and my shield; in him my heart trusts, and I am helped; my heart exults, and with my song I give thanks to him.
>
> —Psalm 28:7, ESV

Your Six Minutes:
What Is God Saying to You Today?

God, where am I overthinking, or in what areas am I trying to hold things in my hands instead of placing them in Yours? Show me, and help me let go.

Day 21

A Word from God on

Remembrance Stones

Look back in remembrance of where we have come together. I've always been near.

> These stones are to be a memorial to the people of Israel forever.
>
> —Joshua 4:7

> Yet this I call to mind and therefore I have hope: Because of the LORD's great love we are not consumed, for his compassions never fail. They are new every morning; great is your faithfulness.
>
> —Lamentations 3:21–23

God, sometimes present struggles can skew my perspective, and I easily forget past victories. Remind me of all the ways You have shown Yourself faithful to me so that I may rejoice, knowing that as You have seen me through before, You will see me through again.

Day 22

A Word from God on

Purpose

You are where I have placed you, and I have given you My authority. Own the place where I have put you, because I have given it to you to steward well. Continue to defer to Me, and your path will grow increasingly bright; your spot, your square, will increase and shine for Me.

I tell you the truth, if you had faith even as small as a mustard seed, you could say to this mountain, "Move from here to there," and it would move. Nothing would be impossible.

—Matthew 17:20, NLT

God, what is my purpose in this season of my life? How am I nurturing it, and in what ways could I better steward the plot You've given me to tend?

A Word from God on

Responding to Difficult Situations Well

Focus on not being reactive, where your responses to situations default to your fleshly, initial reactions. If they get louder, you get quieter. Your authority isn't in the loudness of your voice. Jesus never had to raise His voice to make His point. Even the wind and waves obeyed Him. Submit your wind and waves to Jesus. He calms the storm around and within, and says, "Peace, be still" (Mark 4:39). Jesus didn't respond out of fear or anxiety, because He was confident in His authority and wasn't concerned about having to prove it to anyone.

- He spoke the truth (John 14:6).
- He walked in authority (Matthew 28:18; 7:29).
- He never reacted out of fear (Matthew 6:25–26).
- He served, and He gave (Matthew 20:28).
- He called out and dealt with the enemy and his schemes (Matthew 16:23).
- He was not distracted from His purpose (John 6:38).

A soft answer turns away wrath, but a harsh word stirs up anger. The tongue of the wise commends knowledge, but the mouths of fools pour out folly.

—Proverbs 15:1–2, ESV

And [Jesus] awoke and rebuked the wind and said to the sea, "Peace! Be still!" And the wind ceased, and there was a great calm.

—Mark 4:39, ESV

God, what motivation lies behind my rash responses? Fear? Pride? What is the root issue? Show me how to turn to You in these moments and to usher in Your peace.

Day 24

A Word from God on

Prayer Requests

I am in the process of answering your prayers. From the moment you brought them before Me, I began to act, and I have the solution; they are in progress, and a way will be made. A lesson will be learned, and I know this stretched you, My child. I will make a way where there seems to be no way.

> Then [the messenger from God] said, "Don't be afraid, Daniel. Since the first day you began to pray for understanding and to humble yourself before your God, your request has been heard in heaven. I have come in answer to your prayer. But for twenty-one days the spirit prince of the kingdom of Persia blocked my way. Then Michael, one of the archangels, came to help me, and I left him there with the spirit prince of the kingdom of Persia. Now I am here to explain what will happen to your people in the future, for this vision concerns a time yet to come."
>
> —Daniel 10:12–14, NLT

> But in my distress, I cried out to the LORD; yes, I prayed to my God for help. He heard me from his sanctuary; my cry to him reached his ears. . . . He reached down from heaven and rescued me; he drew me out of deep waters. He rescued me from my powerful enemies, from those who hated me and were too strong for me. They attacked me at a moment when I was in distress, but the LORD supported me. He led me to a place of safety; he rescued me because he delights in me.
>
> —Psalm 18:6, 16–19, NLT

God, am I praying by faith, knowing You will answer my prayers perfectly and not according to my will but Yours? What bold prayers have I left unsaid, ones You are calling me to bring forth and believe for the impossible?

Day 25

A Word from God on

Our True Enemy

The devil has already been defeated once and for all time. He's all bark and no bite. Barks get louder as a dog feels threatened, so don't let the noise intimidate you.

> Be sober-minded; be watchful. Your adversary the devil prowls around like a roaring lion, seeking someone to devour. Resist him, firm in your faith, knowing that the same kinds of suffering are being experienced by your brotherhood throughout the world. And after you have suffered a little while, the God of all grace, who has called you to his eternal glory in Christ, will himself restore, confirm, strengthen, and establish you. To him be the dominion forever and ever. Amen.
>
> —1 Peter 5:8–11, ESV

> Put on the whole armor of God, that you may be able to stand against the schemes of the devil. For we wrestle not against flesh and blood, but against the rulers, against the authorities, against the cosmic powers over this present darkness, against the spiritual forces of evil in the heavenly places. Therefore take up the whole armor of God, that you may be able to withstand in the evil day, and having done all, to stand firm.
>
> —Ephesians 6:11–13, ESV

God, are there fights I'm in where I'm aiming my arrows at the wrong target? What battles do I need to soberly reassess? Help me put my holy game face on and fight the good fight.

Day 26

His Love, Lordship, and Light

I am the Lord in your life, in your kids' lives, in friends' and strangers' lives. Share My love and lordship with all you encounter that they may see and glorify Me.

> You are the light of the world. A town built on a hill cannot be hidden. Neither do people light a lamp and put it under a bowl. Instead they put it on its stand, and it gives light to everyone in the house. In the same way, let your light shine before others, that they may see your good deeds and glorify your Father in heaven.
>
> —Matthew 5:14–16

God, how can I be more intentional, making the most of every situation to shine more brightly for You? Are there talents and abilities You've given me that make my light unique? How can I leverage my gifts and talents to shine for You?

Day 27

Kids

Think of life from your kids' perspective (or that of kids in your life), from their limited knowledge and dependence on you. Let that stir a tenderness and empathy. Offer more hugs, touches, and listening, and less barking orders. Be interested in what interests them. Ten years from now the grades won't matter. Ensure they don't feel as though your love comes at a price or as if a threshold must be met. Extend grace. As I have given to you, give it out. They will fall; they will mess up, and that is part of why they have you. Remember what these ages are like for them. Verbalize and show your unconditional love.

> And they were bringing children to him that he might touch them, and the disciples rebuked them. But when Jesus saw it, he was indignant and said to them, "Let the children come to me; do not hinder them, for to such belongs the kingdom of God. Truly, I say to you, whoever does not receive the kingdom of God like a child shall not enter it." And he took them in his arms and blessed them, laying his hands on them.
>
> —Mark 10:13–16, ESV

Lord Jesus, am I pushing the very ones away that You, in the midst of literally saving the world, stopped to embrace and bless? What mattered to them mattered to You. How can I be more like You in my interactions with my kids or other kids in my life?

Day 28

A Word from God on

Gatekeeping

Do not give way to the enemy, who disguises himself as an angel of light. Stand your ground with what is watched, played with, and heard within your home. Your home is the Lord's. What He says, goes, and what He says, stays. Be on the lookout for anything that opposes the Lord in your home. It is far better to be a friend of God and an enemy of the world than vice versa.

And do not give the devil a foothold.

—Ephesians 4:27

Your Six Minutes:
What Is God Saying to You Today?

God, are there areas in my life I need to clean up? Are there things in my house I need to clean out?

Day 29

A Word from God on

Stillness

"Be still, and know that I am God" (Psalm 46:10). When you feel the pressure to rush and are overwhelmed by the duties of the day, get still before Me. Bring Me into your situation, and gain a heavenly perspective. I am with you always, in all circumstances. Let Me be God in all your life and world. Consult Me and lean in to Me. Run to Me as your strong and fortified tower. Nothing is impossible with Me.

> Why are you cast down, O my soul? And why are you disquieted within me? Hope in God; for I shall yet praise Him, the help of my countenance and my God.
>
> —Psalm 42:11, NKJV

God, what situations do You want to highlight where I could benefit from a more heavenly perspective? What is that perspective, and what do You have to say about that circumstance, person, or problem?

Day 30

A Word from God on

Long-Suffering

Patience and long-suffering are needed when stuff doesn't perfectly align or make sense. Don't expect perfect days; they don't exist in this world. But with My help, you can remain calm in the midst of chaos. Pause. Breathe. Gain perspective. Whatever it is will pass and is probably so fleeting that it's not worth losing your joy and peace over. Think of the impression you leave on others. Would it speak to them to see you stay calm even in the toughest or most surprising situations? That alone would speak volumes. You can do it with My help. Practice today.

And after you have suffered a little while, the God of all grace, who has called you to his eternal glory in Christ, will himself restore, confirm, strengthen, and establish you.

—1 Peter 5:10, ESV

God, in what practical circumstances do I find myself where I can practice waiting well? What would You have me do in the moments when I feel my patience is dwindling?

Day 31

A Word from God on

The Best Investment

Be an investor in people. Take note; focus outside of yourself. Ask people questions that open the door for opportunities to share My love. Remember, all people are My children, and they will know you are Mine by your love. Show off My love.

> A new command I give you: Love one another. As I have loved you, so you must love one another. By this everyone will know that you are my disciples, if you love one another.
>
> —John 13:34–35

God, how can I be more intentional in sharing Your love with others?

Day 32

A Word from God on

Help

As I am an ever-present help to you, be an ever-present help to others. Jesus never said, "I'm too busy." Look for ways to help, encourage, and bless others.

> God is our refuge and strength, a very present help in trouble.
> —Psalm 46:1, ESV

> Do not withhold good from those who deserve it when it's in your power to help them. If you can help your neighbor now, don't say, "Come back tomorrow, and then I'll help you."
> —Proverbs 3:27–28, NLT

God, whom can I help today?

Day 33

Witnessing

A great way to open the door of opportunity and share My love with others is to ask, "How are you today?" Make it a habit to ask this question of everyone with whom you come in contact. This opens the door to a response. Really listen to and care about their response, and ask Me to counsel you on how to respond in return. This is a great practice, and you will get better and bolder as you continually incorporate this into your life.

Don't be surprised by fiery trials; don't let them cultivate fear. They are common for influential kingdom members. They don't surprise Me, and I will always come through for you.

> Honor Christ and let him be the Lord of your life. Always be ready to give an answer when someone asks you about your hope.
>
> —1 Peter 3:15, CEV

> Beloved, do not be surprised at the fiery trial when it comes upon you to test you, as though something strange were happening to you. But rejoice insofar as you share Christ's sufferings, that you may also rejoice and be glad when his glory is revealed.
>
> —1 Peter 4:12–13, ESV

In what daily instances can I use this tactic? Is fear keeping me from witnessing? If so, God, what do You have to say about that?

Day 34

Loving Well

Are you loving people well? Key questions you can ask yourself in any situation are: "Is it loving? Am I operating from a place of love right now?" It's really that simple and powerful. Don't negate the power of love. Love is selfless; love is sacrifice. Love takes effort and intentionality. Love sets a high bar and believes in people. Love roots for people. Love can take a hit and bounce back, because if we fall, we land on the foundation of God's love. Love is truthful. Love is the currency of heaven. Bring it to earth.

If I speak in the tongues of men and of angels, but have not love, I am a noisy gong or a clanging cymbal. And if I have prophetic powers, and understand all mysteries and all knowledge, and if I have all faith, so as to remove mountains, but have not love, I am nothing.

If I give away all I have, and if I deliver up my body to be burned, but have not love, I gain nothing. Love is patient and kind; love does not envy or boast; it is not arrogant or rude. It does not insist on its own way; it is not irritable or resentful; it does not rejoice at wrongdoing, but rejoices with the truth. Love bears all things, believes all things, hopes all things, endures all things.

Love never ends. As for prophecies, they will pass away; as for tongues, they will cease; as for knowledge, it will pass away. For we know in part and we prophesy in part, but when the perfect comes, the partial will pass away. When I was a child, I spoke like a child, I thought like a child, I reasoned like a child. When I became a man, I gave up childish ways. For now we see in a mirror dimly, but then face to face. Now I know in part; then I shall know fully, even as I have been fully known.

So now faith, hope, and love abide, these three; but the greatest of these is love.

—1 Corinthians 13:1–13, ESV

Where do I have room to grow in how I love others? Is there a certain person or difficult situation that comes to mind?

Day 35

A Word from God on

Thoughts and Distractions

Quiet your thoughts. Take heed of where they lead you. Capture and rid yourself of thoughts that are self-serving or skew your perspective. Be mindful of how you spend your time, not letting distractions like the phone steal time with others or sleep. Your time is too precious and too costly for that. Your days will go better if you prioritize sleep. Others will notice your habits and be influenced by them, so there is all the more reason to make good, healthy habits.

We demolish arguments and every pretension that sets itself up against the knowledge of God, and we take captive every thought to make it obedient to Christ.

—2 Corinthians 10:5

Holy Spirit, I need my head examined. Reveal to me what is taking up real estate there, and help me conduct an inventory. What do I need to rid my thoughts of, and what thoughts do I need to make more room for?

Day 36

A Word from God on

Grounding

You are rooted, planted, and grounded. Let no one and nothing uproot you. Stay connected to the Vine, the power source that is always reliable, steady, and secure. Days are unpredictable, but I am not. Become more like Me by being secure, steadfast, and unshaken by the stuff that shakes, because the unshakable remains. Storms come, winds blow, but the boat that is anchored stays put and does not capsize.

> I am the vine; you are the branches. If you remain in me and I in you, you will bear much fruit; apart from me you can do nothing.
>
> —Jesus (John 15:5)

> This means that all of creation will be shaken and removed, so that only unshakable things will remain.
>
> —Hebrews 12:27, NLT

Am I receiving my nutrients from the right source to grow deep spiritual roots? Am I letting You do a complete work in me so that I am breaking new ground, maturing, and producing fruit?

Day 37

Forgiveness

I forgive you, My child. I just want the best for you; please trust Me in this. Trust that I will grant you the desires of your heart. *Trust Me.* You know I know best, and I say these things and provide boundaries for your good. Now don't let the devil kick you and keep you down. Rise up and take your rightful position. You didn't earn it—My Son did that for you. So please don't forsake His gift. Thank Me by honoring and glorifying Me with your life, your thoughts, your choices, your words, and your intentional living. Show the love of God today. The world needs the gift inside of you; don't hide it.

> All this is from God, who reconciled us to himself through Christ and gave us the ministry of reconciliation: that God was reconciling the world to himself in Christ, not counting people's sins against them. And he has committed to us the message of reconciliation. We are therefore Christ's ambassadors, as though God were making his appeal through us. We implore you on Christ's behalf: Be reconciled to God. God made him who had no sin to be sin for us, so that in him we might become the righteousness of God.
>
> —2 Corinthians 5:18–21

God, are there ways I am still trying to earn Your love and forgiveness? Are there ways I, in turn, make others earn my love and forgiveness? What do You have to say about both scenarios? Please grant me a new revelation as to the magnitude of Your love and mercy.

Day 38

A Word from God on

God, Our Fortress

Like a high tower, I keep you safe when you come to Me. Bring all your stuff with you, and leave it with Me! I've got it, and I've got you. Come to Me with all of it throughout your day. Consult with Me in every interaction; walk with intention and integrity; and watch how I will make a way for you. You don't need to self-advocate; you have an advocate and an intercessor in Me.

> The name of the LORD is a strong tower; the righteous run to it and are safe.
>
> —Proverbs 18:10, NKJV

God, help me dwell with You and consider how You care for me. God, what do I continue to try to handle myself that You are asking me to lay down?

Day 39

A Word from God on

The Fruit of the Spirit

Choose life in your thoughts, words, actions, and reactions. Give grace. Show patience. Show off those attractive fruits of the Spirit.

- Love: Be loving and lovable.
- Joy: Be joyful.
- Peace: Be peaceful and advocate for peace.
- Patience: Be patient.
- Kindness: Be kind.
- Goodness: Be good.
- Faithfulness: Be faithful. Show up again and again.
- Gentleness: Be gentle, especially with people.
- Self-control: Exercise self-control.

You can do all things through Christ who strengthens you. Don't let the devil tell you that you can't.

You, my brothers and sisters, were called to be free. But do not use your freedom to indulge the flesh; rather, serve one another humbly in love. For the entire law is fulfilled in keeping this one command: "Love your neighbor as yourself." If you bite and devour each other, watch out or you will be destroyed by each other.

So I say, walk by the Spirit, and you will not gratify the desires of the flesh. For the flesh desires what is contrary to the Spirit, and the Spirit what is contrary to the flesh. They are in conflict with each other, so that you are not to do whatever you want. But if you are led by the Spirit, you are not under the law.

The acts of the flesh are obvious: sexual immorality, impurity and debauchery; idolatry and witchcraft; hatred, discord, jealousy, fits of rage, selfish ambition, dissensions, factions and envy; drunkenness, orgies, and the like. I warn you, as I did before, that those who live like this will not inherit the kingdom of God.

But the fruit of the Spirit is love, joy, peace, forbearance, kindness, goodness, faithfulness, gentleness and self-control. Against such things there is no law. Those who belong to Christ Jesus have crucified the flesh with its passions and desires. Since we live by the Spirit, let us keep in step with the Spirit.

—Galatians 5:13–25

God, I know this is not the time for self-assessment, and You don't judge me according to my performance, and for that I am forever grateful. Holy Spirit, I instead ask You to search me and know me and reveal Your fruit to me in a new way. What do You have to say about bearing Your fruit?

Day 40

A Word from God on

Renewal

Break up the fallow ground. Sow for yourself righteousness. Reap steadfast love. Break up your fallow ground, for it's time to seek Me so that I may come and rain righteousness upon you. Do not sow your seeds among thorns.

Note: Fallow ground is land that has been left unplowed and unseeded *during a growing season*. This farming technique allows the land to recover, store organic matter, and retain moisture. Fallowing also disrupts the life cycle of pests and pathogens by temporarily removing their hosts.[1]

Sometimes land grows fallow due to neglect, and sometimes the fallowing, or pausing in working the land, is actually done on purpose. In the season of waiting, when it looks like nothing is happening, recovery is occurring, pests are removed, and vital nutrients are restored. The amazing thing is that God is so gracious and merciful that He doesn't waste it either way! Whether the land of our hearts has grown fallow because of our own willful disobedience and neglect, or because God called us to a season of purposeful rest and waiting, He manages to bring good out of it if we, in the end, turn it over to Him, return to Him, seek Him, and break up what needs breaking when He calls us to act.

> "If you, Israel, will return, then return to me," declares the LORD. "If you put your detestable idols out of my sight and no longer go astray, and if in a truthful, just and righteous way you swear, 'As surely as the LORD lives,' then the nations will invoke blessings by him and in him they will boast." This is what the LORD says to the people of Judah and to Jerusalem: "Break up your unplowed ground and do not sow among thorns. Circumcise yourselves to the LORD, circumcise your hearts."
> —Jeremiah 4:1–4

1. Darcy Larum, "What Is Fallow Ground: Are There Any Benefits of Fallowing Soil," Gardening Know How, August 13, 2018, https://www.gardeningknowhow.com/garden -how-to/soil-fertilizers/what-is-fallow-ground.htm.

God, are You calling me to a resting season or an action season? You may be telling me to act in one area and rest in another, for only You know! Please show me what Your will is for me in this season, and help me be obedient.

Day 41

A Word from God on

The Secret Place

I have a good plan for you. Come away with Me to the secret place. I reveal My secrets to My friends. Draw near. Be content with Me alone, and you will be rewarded and refreshed. In My presence, there is fullness of joy. My peace I give to you, but not as the world gives. I will pour out My blessing upon you so abundantly that you will not have room to contain it. This is My will: that from the overflow you may spread My blessings to those around you. That's kingdom business: fruit that remains and a heritage that lasts.

> You are my friends if you do what I command. I no longer call you slaves, because a master doesn't confide in his slaves. Now you are my friends, since I have told you everything the Father told me.
>
> —John 15:14–15, NLT

> But it was to us that God revealed these things by his Spirit. For his Spirit searches out everything and shows us God's deep secrets.
>
> —1 Corinthians 2:10, NLT

> You make known to me the path of life; in your presence there is fullness of joy; at your right hand are pleasures forevermore.
>
> —Psalm 16:11, ESV

God, help me quiet my thoughts so I can hear Your thoughts. Thank You that You desire to share Your secrets, Your ways, and Your intents with those who seek You. What do You desire to show me today? What blessings have I already received that I can share with others and take part in kingdom business? Please help me see how I have been blessed and how to be a blessing.

A Word from God on

Knowing Him

When you search for Me, you find and get to know Me. When you know someone, you can defend their character because of your personal relationship, beyond what others say. You are a character witness for God.

> "For I know the plans I have for you," declares the LORD, "plans to prosper you and not to harm you, plans to give you hope and a future. Then you will call on me and come and pray to me, and I will listen to you. You will seek me and find me when you seek me with all your heart. I will be found by you," declares the LORD.
>
> —Jeremiah 29:11–14

Holy Spirit, bring to remembrance the key times in my life You have revealed Your nature to me through firsthand experience. What did those times show me about Your character? How can I use these experiences to serve others and introduce them to You?

Day 43

A Word from God on

Obedience

Lay hold of that which I place before you. You are storing up treasure in heaven. Thank you for being obedient. I'm proud of you. Now you have true peace that comes from walking in unity with Me. How can two walk together unless they are agreed? Together we will go far and accomplish much; wait and see! I will fortify and protect you. Nothing shall by any means harm you (Luke 10:19). Seek first My kingdom and My righteousness, and all these things will be added unto you (Matthew 6:33).

> I press on to take hold of that for which Christ Jesus took hold of me. Brothers and sisters, I do not consider myself yet to have taken hold of it. But one thing I do: Forgetting what is behind and straining toward what is ahead, I press on toward the goal to win the prize for which God has called me heavenward in Christ Jesus.
>
> —Philippians 3:12–14

> Can two walk together, unless they are agreed?
>
> —Amos 3:3, NKJV

> Do not store up for yourselves treasures on earth, where moths and vermin destroy, and where thieves break in and steal. But store up for yourselves treasures in heaven, where moths and vermin do not destroy, and where thieves do not break in and steal. For where your treasure is, there your heart will be also.
>
> —Matthew 6:19–21

God, I can only walk in step with You and ensure I'm going in the right direction by submitting myself to Your navigation. Am I doing that? Where am I now? Where am I headed? Do I need a course correction?

Day 44

A Word from God on

Purpose

Everything I do is on purpose. I don't waste anything. You were intentionally created. I wanted you on the earth, knowing it wouldn't be the same without you. I thought it through, beginning to end, as I planned and paved the way I had in mind for you. I created who you are with the same beautiful intention.

> For you created my inmost being; you knit me together in my mother's womb. I praise you because I am fearfully and wonderfully made; your works are wonderful, I know that full well. My frame was not hidden from you when I was made in the secret place, when I was woven together in the depths of the earth. Your eyes saw my unformed body; all the days ordained for me were written in your book before one of them came to be. How precious to me are your thoughts, God! How vast is the sum of them!
>
> —Psalm 139:13–17

God, how it must grieve Your heart when I fail to value what You care about, including myself and others. What do You want me to know about how You see and value me? Is there someone You want me to view differently? Give me supernatural vision to glimpse how You see them so I can view them through Your eyes.

Day 45

A Word from God on

A New Way to Go

The old has gone; the new has come. I am doing something new; do you not perceive it? As you fear Me, I call you (in obedience to Me) to honor, respect, and love My people. You can't fear Me and not love My people. Watch your words because they steer the whole ship. So, where do you want the ship to go? The ship needs to stay afloat and go in the right direction. Think of your words as arrows pointing where you want things to go!

> Indeed, we all make many mistakes. For if we could control our tongues, we would be perfect and could also control ourselves in every other way. We can make a large horse go wherever we want by means of a small bit in its mouth. And a small rudder makes a huge ship turn wherever the pilot chooses to go, even though the winds are strong. In the same way, the tongue is a small thing that makes grand speeches. But a tiny spark can set a great forest on fire.

> But the wisdom from above is first of all pure. It is also peace loving, gentle at all times, and willing to yield to others. It is full of mercy and the fruit of good deeds. It shows no favoritism and is always sincere. And those who are peacemakers will plant seeds of peace and reap a harvest of righteousness.
>
> —James 3:2–5, 17–18, NLT

Lord, what sort of seeds am I planting with my words? Am I sowing carefully to ensure I'm producing a desirable crop? God, what do You have to say about my words and behavior? What words and actions need pruning? Holy Spirit, show me what it looks like to live that out.

Day 46

A Word from God on

Growth

Strengthen yourself in Me, as David did. He learned how to do this *before* he was king and continued in both good times and bad. Be faithful in the small things so that I can entrust you with more. Be strengthened and reinforced. Stand firm on the platform I've given you. I put you where you are, not any man. What I plan, I protect.

> The Lord who rescued me from the paw of the lion and the paw of the bear will rescue me from the hand of this Philistine.
>
> —1 Samuel 17:37

David was not afraid to face Goliath, because he learned how to trust God while encountering trials during his days as a boy tending sheep.

> And David was greatly distressed, for the people spoke of stoning him, because all the people were bitter in soul, each for his sons and daughters. But David strengthened himself in the Lord his God.
>
> —1 Samuel 30:6, ESV

> Do not despise these small beginnings, for the Lord rejoices to see the work begin.
>
> —Zechariah 4:10, NLT

Are there responsibilities that I don't feel qualified to handle or that I'm in over my head with? God, what do You have to say about those? Am I truly trusting You to help me? What does it look like to trust You in something versus not trusting You? What do You have to say about the things on my plate? Where am I, and where am I headed?

A Word from God on

Standing Up and Standing Out

In a world of darkness, be the light. Stand out. Be different, and get comfortable in it. Don't murmur, don't complain, don't compare, don't judge, don't assume, don't pretend, don't cast out, and don't look the other way. Look right in the face of evil and overpower it with love. Don't back down, and don't give up. Press on, press in, and stay the course. Eyes on Me; I *won't* steer you wrong. Plant your feet, grow roots, chart a course, and let Me guide the way. Let's go.

Love must be sincere. Hate what is evil; cling to what is good. . . . Never be lacking in zeal, but keep your spiritual fervor, serving the Lord. Be joyful in hope, patient in affliction, faithful in prayer. . . . Bless those who persecute you; bless and do not curse. . . . Do not be overcome by evil, but overcome evil with good.

—Romans 12:9, 11–12, 14, 21

Let your light shine before others, that they may see your good deeds and glorify your Father in heaven.

—Matthew 5:16

Your Six Minutes:
What Is God Saying to You Today?

Lord, in what ways am I blending in, and in what ways am I standing out? What are You illuminating as I take stock of my day-to-day life? What do You want to reveal to me about my habits and routines, my default responses, and the way I conduct myself?

Day 48

A Word from God on

Humble Pie

If anything is motivated by pride or getting the upper hand, squash it and humble yourself immediately. Trust Me to speak on your behalf and give you favor where needed. Remember, you don't have to do everything and exhaust yourself trying to make things happen. Let go and let God. Bring Me your desires and your needs. You stand as an advocate for many, but bring your appeals to Me, and I will appeal to others on your behalf. Pause before acting so I can show you when to speak and move, and when to keep silent and still.

So humble yourselves under the mighty power of God, and at the right time he will lift you up in honor. Give all your worries and cares to God, for he cares about you.

—1 Peter 5:6–7, NLT

Are my actions or decisions based on pride? God, I want to do the right things for the right reasons, to bring You glory and not for self-preservation. Show me what to let go of and where I may need a perspective shift.

Day 49

Speaking Up

I've given you a voice for a reason. Use it for Me. Win many to Me; join the adventure.

> But how can they call on him to save them unless they believe in him? And how can they believe in him if they have never heard about him? And how can they hear about him unless someone tells them?
> —Romans 10:14, NLT

> You yourselves are our letter, written on our hearts, known and read by everyone. You show that you are a letter from Christ, the result of our ministry, written not with ink but with the Spirit of the living God, not on tablets of stone but on tablets of human hearts.
> —2 Corinthians 3:2–3

God, is there someone I need to tell about You? How can I share the gospel in my everyday life?

Day 50

A Word from God on

Stepping Out

Speak to the mountain, and it will move. My plans, *Mine*, will come to pass. Jesus declared and commanded the winds and waves to be still. Right now you're on a boat, away from solid ground, because you had to step off the shore to get to the other side. There are risks involved, and it's not as safe as dry land, but it's necessary to get to where I'm leading you. Be encouraged! Jesus is with you, and He isn't worried. He knows the way and will ensure you reach the other side. With Jesus' help, every storm can be silenced. Keep going.

> I will instruct you and teach you in the way you should go; I will counsel you with my loving eye on you.
>
> —Psalm 32:8

> When He [Jesus] had stopped speaking, He said to Simon, "Launch out into the deep and let down your nets for a catch."
>
> —Luke 5:4, NKJV

Lord, are there areas where I've doubted Your faithfulness because the path got bumpy? What do You want to say about those circumstances?

A Word from God on

Hidden Treasure

Sift through the rubble to find the treasures. Digging is required. Listen. Lean in. Encourage.

> For God, who said, "Let light shine out of darkness," made his light shine in our hearts to give us the light of the knowledge of God's glory displayed in the face of Christ. But we have this treasure in jars of clay to show that this all-surpassing power is from God and not from us.
>
> —2 Corinthians 4:6–7

God, are there people whose treasure I've overlooked? Are there areas where I need a perspective shift to see the hidden treasure in the ordinary or seemingly unattractive?

Day 52

Unloading

I don't cause overwhelm (as in more than you can bear); that is not from Me. Anytime that feeling comes upon you, acknowledge it for what it is, bring it to Me, and ask for guidance on how to practically assess the why behind the emotion. What is in your control to change, and what is not? How can you make the most of the situation without letting the feeling of dread overrule truth? The truth is that you are well cared for by Me; you are fully loved by Me; you are a work in progress and *are* progressing. The truth is, I can answer any need and squash any lie. My light outshines the darkness that feels powerful and intimidating. Love carries more power and weight than any external force. Cling to the basics. Come back to the fruit of the Spirit, which overrides law and performance.

I have learned how to be content with whatever I have. I know how to live on almost nothing or with everything. I have learned the secret of living in every situation, whether it is with a full stomach or empty, with plenty or little. For I can do everything through Christ, who gives me strength.

—Philippians 4:11–13, NLT

But the fruit of the Spirit is love, joy, peace, forbearance, kindness, goodness, faithfulness, gentleness and self-control. Against such things there is no law.

—Galatians 5:22–23

Come to Me, all you who labor and are heavy laden, and I will give you rest. Take My yoke upon you and learn from Me, for I am gentle and lowly in heart, and you will find rest for your souls. For My yoke is easy and My burden is light.

—Matthew 11:28–30, NKJV

No temptation has overtaken you except such as is common to man; but God is faithful, who will not allow you to be tempted beyond what you are able, but with the temptation will also make the way of escape, that you may be able to bear it.

—1 Corinthians 10:13, NKJV

God, what lies have I let creep in that may be stealing my peace? What truths do You want to replace them with?

Day 53

Isaiah 60

We have been redeemed; a pleasing sacrifice was approved on our behalf on the altar. When there is darkness all around, God has entrusted us with His light as it shines from within us. Where there is despair, we have an everlasting hope. What man may have rejected, God has redeemed and called His own.

Redeemed means to purchase back; to ransom; to liberate or rescue from captivity or bondage; to repurchase what has been sold; to regain possession of a thing alienated.[1]

> Arise, shine, for your light has come, and the glory of the LORD rises upon you. See, darkness covers the earth and thick darkness is over the peoples, but the LORD rises upon you and his glory appears over you.
> —Isaiah 60:1–2

> For we are His workmanship, created in Christ Jesus for good works, which God prepared beforehand that we should walk in them.
> —Ephesians 2:10, NKJV

> You are the light of the world. A city that is set on a hill cannot be hidden. Nor do they light a lamp and put it under a basket, but on a lampstand, and it gives light to all who are in the house.
> —Matthew 5:14–15, NKJV

---

1. Travis Bradberry, "Emotional Intelligence 2.0 Step by Step," TalentSmartEQ, November 4, 2024, https://www.talentsmarteq.com/emotional-intelligence-2-0-step-by-step/.

Lord, You bought me at a high price. You counted the cost for all those around me too. Give me new insight to really grasp this truth. What are You speaking to my heart regarding what this means?

Day 54

A Word from God on

Rest

Come rest in Me. Even in work and movement, your soul (your mind, will, and emotions) can rest in Me. Fellowship with Me; commune with Me. Enjoy the fellowship of My company. I love spending time with you.

The first scripture is f rom the parable of the lost son, an allegory of God's love for us.

> While he was still a long way off, his father saw him and was filled with compassion for him; he ran to his son, threw his arms around him and kissed him.
>
> —Luke 15:20

> Come to Me, all you who labor and are heavy laden, and I will give you rest.
>
> —Matthew 11:28, NKJV

> The LORD is my shepherd; I shall not want. He makes me to lie down in green pastures; He leads me beside the still waters. He restores my soul; He leads me in the paths of righteousness for His name's sake.
>
> —Psalm 23:1–3, NKJV

Lord, let me curl up in Your lap, feel Your embrace, and hear what You want to whisper to me.

A Word from God on

Vision and Fixing Your Eyes

Where there is no vision, My people perish (Proverbs 29:18). Write the vision, and make it plain (Habakkuk 2:2). I have come that they might have life to the full (John 10:10) and enjoy it. Life, peace, and prosperity in all you do is yours today and every day. I don't give as the world gives (John 14:27), so don't look to the things of this world for answers and solutions. Look to Me, you who toils, and I will give you rest and My shalom (peace), nothing missing, nothing broken.

> Where there is no vision, the people perish: but he that keepeth the law, happy is he.
>
> —Proverbs 29:18, KJV

> The thief cometh not, but that he may steal, and kill, and destroy: I came that they may have life, and may have it abundantly.
>
> —John 10:10, ASV

> Peace I leave with you; my peace I give you. I do not give to you as the world gives. Do not let your hearts be troubled and do not be afraid.
>
> —John 14:27

Lord, open my eyes to see life the way You intend it for me, setting my vision to align with You and what is significant in Your eyes. Where do I need to shift my focus, stop toiling, and start receiving from Your streams of living water and abundance?

Day 56

A Word from God on

Peace, Part 1

My children can remain in peace regardless of their circumstances because the peace I give is not dependent on the conditions but is stable, fixed, and always available for you to take hold of. This means that what would cause others to lose their peace shouldn't cause the same for you, because peace is not a denial of the facts but an absolute faith in the truth from an eternal perspective. You can have peace as you remember I am your waymaker. Your needs are met according to My abundance. Unusual favor is yours.

> Don't worry about anything; instead, pray about everything. Tell God what you need, and thank him for all he has done. Then you will experience God's peace, which exceeds anything we can understand. His peace will guard your hearts and minds as you live in Christ Jesus.
> —Philippians 4:6–7, NLT

> And this same God who takes care of me will supply all your needs from his glorious riches, which have been given to us in Christ Jesus.
> —Philippians 4:19, NLT

> And let the peace (soul harmony which comes) from Christ rule (act as umpire continually) in your hearts [deciding and settling with finality all questions that arise in your minds, in that peaceful state] to which as [members of Christ's] one body you were also called [to live]. And be thankful (appreciative), [giving praise to God always].
> —Colossians 3:15, AMPC

God, how can I keep my peace in ____________, at ____________, or with ____________? Holy Spirit, please give me a supernatural strategy.

A Word from God on

Peace, Part 2

No matter what is going on, you can have My peace. You can act in My peace; you can think in My peace and move in My peace. I said it because it is possible. The devil is a liar, so do not look at him or entertain him. Eyes on Me, cares on Me, and I will hold you and see you through to victory together.

How about we start today? No more running around in circles, giving in to the same temptation of panicking and losing your cool. Every challenge is a test to get it right. I do not give tests thinking you will fail. I give them knowing you can do it and succeed because with Me you can. Don't go it alone; do it with Me. Together we've got this. The cross wasn't too much for Me, and this isn't either.

> Fear not, for I am with you; be not dismayed, for I am your God; I will strengthen you, I will help you, I will uphold you with my righteous right hand.
>
> —Isaiah 41:10, ESV

God, a full day of holding on to peace as the treasure is so foreign to me. I know peace doesn't mean a life without challenges or obstacles, but it's a game-changing mindset and takes intentional submission to You. I commit to surrendering this day fully to You. What do You want me to be mindful of as I embark upon this day?

Day 58

A Word from God on

Perspective

Look from My perspective. Do I have a solution? Have I approved you? Is My approval based on your works? I approve of you, and I've set you in your place. What God has placed, man cannot replace.

> Remember not the former things, nor consider the things of old. Behold, I am doing a new thing; now it springs forth, do you not perceive it? I will make a way in the wilderness and rivers in the desert.
>
> —Isaiah 43:18–19, ESV

> For the LORD does not see as man sees; for man looks at the outward appearance, but the LORD looks at the heart.
>
> —1 Samuel 16:7, NKJV

Your Six Minutes:
What Is God Saying to You Today?

God, for every problem, You already have a solution. For all my lack, Jesus already paid the price. Show me and teach me what You want me to see and understand about my situation.

Day 59

A Word from God on

God's Yoke, Part 1

My yoke is easy, and My burden is light, so stay yoked to Me. Surrender control; do things My way. Continually lay down pride. I will help you. Don't rush to respond! When you carry a cross, it's not a sprint, and it's not about speed. It's about making a deliberate choice to put one foot in front of the other. Jesus had to patiently wait for the fulfillment of His calling, but people had to see His journey. There was purpose in it. People had to watch Him carry that cross.

> Come to me, all you who are weary and burdened, and I will give you rest. Take my yoke upon you and learn from me, for I am gentle and humble in heart, and you will find rest for your souls. For my yoke is easy and my burden is light.
>
> —Matthew 11:28–30

God, it can take faith to wait. You are patient; it's the devil who tries to rush us. Where do I need to slow down? Where are You telling me to pause until You make the right response, the right way, or the right words clear to me?

Day 60

A Word from God on

God's Yoke, Part 2

You are yoked to the source of all you need. Like Inspector Gadget, who was able to just say "Go, go gadget," and name the tool he needed, and it appeared (such as a battery pack or a power source), you can ask for what you need. I'm not Santa. You don't always get what you want, but you'll always get what you need. Your needs might look different from what you think. You may ask for a hammer, but I'll give you a flashlight. You might want to pound something, but instead, I need you to gain clarity about what you're ready to pound. What you are ready to destroy still has value, and I need you to see that.

> That is why we never give up. Though our bodies are dying, our spirits are being renewed every day. For our present troubles are small and won't last very long. Yet they produce for us a glory that vastly outweighs them and will last forever! So, we don't look at the troubles we can see now; rather, we fix our gaze on things that cannot be seen. For the things we see now will soon be gone, but the things we cannot see will last forever.
>
> —2 Corinthians 4:16–18, NLT

> Likewise the Spirit helps us in our weakness. For we do not know what to pray for as we ought, but the Spirit himself intercedes for us with groanings too deep for words. And he who searches hearts knows what is the mind of the Spirit, because the Spirit intercedes for the saints according to the will of God. And we know that for those who love God all things work together for good, for those who are called according to his purpose.
>
> —Romans 8:26–28, ESV

> You ask and do not receive, because you ask wrongly, to spend it on your passions.
>
> —James 4:3, ESV

Holy Spirit, please intercede on my behalf before the Father. Show me if You want me to pray differently regarding a situation I am facing or a need I have so that my prayers would align with my Father's will.

Day 61

A Word from God on

Today

I have made *this* day. Rejoice and be glad in it! It is as special to Me as the first day I ever made, and when I made it, I knew all about this day too. I'm trustworthy; I'm faithful. As I saw through that first day and all the days in between, keeping everything aligned and in orbit, I keep this day. It is good. How many of My children have called to Me in distress from a pit of despair between now and then? Consider and remember Job. I was with him even in his darkest moments, and I will be with you too! I've got you; I'm holding you *and* this world.

> I called on the LORD in distress; the LORD answered me and set me in a broad place. The LORD is on my side; I will not fear. What can man do to me? . . . This is the day the LORD has made; we will rejoice and be glad in it.
>
> —Psalm 118:5–6, 24, NKJV

> As you know, we count as blessed those who have persevered. You have heard of Job's perseverance and have seen what the Lord finally brought about. The Lord is full of compassion and mercy.
>
> —James 5:11

God, as I look upon this day, help me see it with fresh eyes. What beauty do You want to reveal to me? Let me sit and enjoy some time with You as You point out Your handiwork all around me.

Day 62

A Word from God on

Breakthrough, Part 1

Do not fear; do not fret. I am the waymaker. Trust Me. Nothing is impossible for Me. Breakthrough is coming.

And the God of all grace, who called you to his eternal glory in Christ, after you have suffered a little while, will himself restore you and make you strong, firm and steadfast.

—1 Peter 5:10

When I think of the primary area of struggle in my life right now, help me, God, thank You through faith, knowing that a breakthrough is coming. Show me what You want me to understand about that situation.

Day 63

Breakthrough, Part 2

Some suffering included. When you bake a cake, the ingredients have to all get mixed into a lumpy mess and go through the heat, but then you end up with a cake!

> And let us not grow weary of doing good, for in due season we will reap, if we do not give up.
>
> —Galatians 6:9, ESV

God, show me how, with whatever part of the process I find myself in, to trust that dessert is coming! Reveal to me a new insight into the purpose You are perfecting.

Day 64

A Word from God on

Breakthrough, Part 3

I am the God of the breakthrough. I will break through that which has been built up like a wall in your way. At the sound of My voice, it falls. I place you on a broad path; keep your eyes on Me, for I have said that at the proper time I, the Lord, will do it.

> Arise. . . . Let your light shine for all to see. For the glory of the Lord rises to shine on you. Darkness as black as night covers all the nations of the earth, but the glory of the Lord rises and appears over you. . . .
>
> I will make peace your leader and righteousness your ruler. . . . Salvation will surround you like city walls, and praise will be on the lips of all who enter here. . . .
>
> All your people will be righteous. They will possess the land forever, for I will plant them there with my own hands in order to bring myself glory. . . . At the right time, I, the Lord, will make this happen.
>
> —Isaiah 60:1–2, 17–18, 21–22, NLT

God, have I been limiting my faith in You and Your ability through the confines of my own reasoning? Your ways are higher than my ways. I know this, God. Reveal to me if there is an area I've doubted Your ability to reach and change. Show me what You have to say about that situation.

Day 65

A Word from God on

The Mind of Christ

You have the mind of Christ and can do all that I call you to do with My help. That means:

- Be careful not to engage in what I haven't called you to.
- Be careful not to try to do what I have called you to do, without Me.

Both are recipes for disaster. Trust Me to guide you day by day. It's a jungle out there, so suit up. Put on love. Dress yourself accordingly.

Colossians 3 (my paraphrase):

- Verse 1: Set your mind on things above
- Verse 3: 'cause you're dead.
- Verse 5: You and all your ugly stuff—
- Verse 8: that's not you anymore, so have nothing to do with that old mess.
- Verse 9: Your new self is with Jesus; it's not just you anymore.
- Verse 14: Put on love, the binding ingredient,
- Verse 15: and let God's peace rule you.

Since, then, you have been raised with Christ, set your hearts on things above, where Christ is, seated at the right hand of God. Set your minds on things above, not on earthly things. For you died, and your life is now hidden with Christ in God. When Christ, who is your life, appears, then you also will appear with him in glory.

Put to death, therefore, whatever belongs to your earthly nature: sexual immorality, impurity, lust, evil desires and greed, which is idolatry. Because of these, the wrath of God is coming. You used to walk in these ways, in the life you once lived. But now you must also rid yourselves of all such things as these: anger, rage, malice, slander, and filthy language from your lips. Do not lie to each other, since you have taken off your old self with its practices and have put on the new self, which is being renewed in knowledge in the image of its Creator. Here there is no Gentile or Jew, circumcised or uncircumcised, barbarian, Scythian, slave or free, but Christ is all, and is in all.

Therefore, as God's chosen people, holy and dearly loved, clothe your-selves with compassion, kindness, humility, gentleness and patience. Bear with each other and forgive one another if any of you has a griev-ance against someone. Forgive as the Lord forgave you. And over all these virtues put on love, which binds them all together in perfect unity.

Let the peace of Christ rule in your hearts, since as members of one body you were called to peace. And be thankful.

—Colossians 3:1–15

For, "Who can know the LORD's thoughts? Who knows enough to teach him?" But we understand these things, for we have the mind of Christ.

—1 Corinthians 2:16, NLT

God, that's a lot to process; what does all this mean? What are You saying to me? What is rising in my spirit as I marinate in Your words?

Day 66

A Word from God on

Following the Leader

Follow My lead; let Me lead. Love Me; love others; love yourself. Love is the secret ingredient. "Be self-controlled and sober-minded for the sake of your prayers" (1 Peter 4:7). Keep loving others earnestly, for love covers a multitude of sins. Do not be surprised at the fiery trials when they come upon you.

> Be self-controlled and sober-minded for the sake of your prayers. Above all, keep loving one another earnestly, since love covers a multitude of sins. . . .

> Therefore let those who suffer according to God's will entrust their souls to a faithful Creator while doing good.

—1 Peter 4:7–8, 19, ESV

God, how am I doing at loving You, others, and myself? Do I keep loving faithfully even when it looks fruitless or amid a trial? Help me recall how Jesus responded to suffering, and show me how to be more like Him.

Day 67

Fatherhood

I've got you, and I've got your kids. I knew you wouldn't be a perfect parent when I gave them to you, and you never will be. Look to Me as your standard and example.

Characteristics of God the Father (to imitate whether we are parents or not):

- Is faithful
- Is just
- Is dependable
- Is trustworthy
- Is approachable
- Is honest
- Desires the best for us
- Teaches right and wrong
- Always points back to the Word and the truth
- Leads by example
- Is not controlling
- Is loving
- Is patient
- Is kind
- Is forgiving
- Doesn't compromise on right and wrong
- Loves all

Every good gift and every perfect gift is from above, coming down from the Father of lights, with whom there is no variation or shadow due to change [He is always the same and consistently good].

—James 1:17, ESV

But he said to me, "My grace is sufficient for you, for my power is made perfect in weakness." Therefore, I will boast all the more gladly of my weaknesses, so that the power of Christ may rest upon me.

—2 Corinthians 12:9, ESV

God, I meditate on these amazing attributes that correct any way I've shortsighted Your character. Reveal to me how this translates to my life, specifically for our relationship. Is there anything that stands out regarding how these traits can be applied in my relationships with my kids or others?

Day 68

A Word from God on

Plans

"I know the plans I have for you . . . plans to prosper you and not to harm you," to give you both a future and a hope, hope that you have a prosperous and not harmful future (Jeremiah 29:11). Yes, hard or challenging times and circumstances come, but I am God over that too. I am watching over you in those times; you can learn from them and trust that you will be all right. In difficult times, if you can remember I'm good and you'll be OK, then you'll be OK! Perseverance builds character, and character, hope.

> "For I know the plans I have for you," declares the LORD, "plans to prosper you and not to harm you, plans to give you hope and a future. Then you will call on me and come and pray to me, and I will listen to you. You will seek me and find me when you seek me with all your heart. I will be found by you," declares the LORD.
>
> —Jeremiah 29:11–14

> We also glory in our sufferings, because we know that suffering produces perseverance; perseverance, character; and character, hope.
>
> —Romans 5:3–4

Hope means to desire with expectation of obtainment or fulfillment; to expect with confidence.[1]

---

1. *Merriam-Webster*, s.v. "hope," accessed December 8, 2025, https://www.merriam -webster.com/dictionary/hope.

God, am I allowing my challenges to change me for the better? Allowing them to build my character, working toward the end result of hope? If I lack hope, it's an indicator I lack trust in You. Inventory me, Lord. Reveal where You are allowing me to persevere so I will trust You in greater measure. Given these truths, help me see my circumstances from a heavenly perspective and with an eternal purpose.

A Word from God on

Hope

Character builds hope because when I come through in the hard times, you learn that I will surely do it again. You are building up stones of remembrance (Joshua 4); there is beauty in the outcome and in the happy ending, but also in the treacherous journey. Job's story would not be remarkable had it not shown how he traversed, pushed through, held on to Me, and continued to ignore the voices around him, but ultimately listened to My voice. That's how he got through it all.

A reminder from yesterday: *Hope* means to desire with expectation of obtainment or fulfillment; to expect with confidence.[1]

> As an example of suffering and patience, brothers, take the prophets who spoke in the name of the Lord. Behold, we consider those blessed who remained steadfast. You have heard of the steadfastness of Job, and you have seen the purpose of the Lord, how the Lord is compassionate and merciful.
>
> —James 5:10–11, ESV

> And they overcame him by the blood of the Lamb and by the word of their testimony.
>
> —Revelation 12:11, NKJV

1. *Merriam-Webster*, s.v. "hope," accessed December 8, 2025, https://www.merriam-webster.com/dictionary/hope.

Lord, recall to my mind past times when You have shown Yourself faithful to me. Reveal how the former tests are my current-day testimony that can serve to bolster my faith in present-day challenges.

Day 70

Walking It Out

Own what is yours. Lead by example. Your actions speak louder than words. If your actions contradict your words, your words lose their value. What does it look like to show love and care beyond saying it?

> Pursue peace with all people, and holiness, without which no one will see the Lord.
>
> —Hebrews 12:14, NKJV

God, what steps can I take today to get outside of myself, put others' needs before my own, and live out Your call to walk in a way that shows off Your love to others?

Day 71

A Word from God on

A Holy Anatomy

Taking up your cross and dying to self doesn't mean you don't matter. You are My instrument, a vital component to the proper working of the body of Christ. But it functions properly only when submitted to the headship of Christ.

> Then Jesus told his disciples, "If anyone would come after me, let him deny himself and take up his cross and follow me. For whoever would save his life will lose it, but whoever loses his life for my sake will find it."
>
> —Matthew 16:24–25, ESV

> Yes, the body has many different parts, not just one part. If the foot says, "I am not a part of the body because I am not a hand," that does not make it any less a part of the body. And if the ear says, "I am not part of the body because I am not an eye," would that make it any less a part of the body? If the whole body were an eye, how would you hear? Or if your whole body were an ear, how would you smell anything?

> But our bodies have many parts, and God has put each part just where he wants it. How strange a body would be if it had only one part! Yes, there are many parts, but only one body. The eye can never say to the hand, "I don't need you." The head can't say to the feet, "I don't need you."

> In fact, some parts of the body that seem weakest and least important are actually the most necessary. And the parts we regard as less honorable are those we clothe with the greatest care. So we carefully protect those parts that should not be seen, while the more honorable parts do not require this special care. So God has put the body together such that extra honor and care are given to those parts that have less dignity. This makes for harmony among the members, so that all the members care for each other. If one part suffers, all the parts suffer with it, and if one part is honored, all the parts are glad.

> All of you together are Christ's body, and each of you is a part of it.
>
> —1 Corinthians 12:14–27, NLT

God, check me if I have been thinking too highly or too lowly of myself. What do You want to say to me about the members of the body of Christ around me? Help me see my brothers and sisters in Christ in a new light, see the beautiful mixture of unique characters that they are.

Day 72

Beginnings and Endings

Finale: the end of something that usually signals the beginning of something else. Often a new thing can't start until another thing ends. Jesus left the earth so the Holy Spirit could come. His followers were brokenhearted and confused, but it was best. Trust Me with every turn, diversion, and end. I will never leave you or forsake you, and My plan remains good.

> Nevertheless, I tell you the truth: it is to your advantage that I go away, for if I do not go away, the Helper [Holy Spirit] will not come to you. But if I go, I will send him to you.
>
> —Jesus (John 16:7, ESV)

> Be strong and courageous. Do not fear or be in dread of them, for it is the LORD your God who goes with you. He will not leave you or forsake you.
>
> —Deuteronomy 31:6, ESV

> "For I know the plans I have for you," declares the LORD, "plans to prosper you and not to harm you, plans to give you hope and a future."
>
> —Jeremiah 29:11

Lord, what do You want to say to me about any transitions I may be facing?

Day 73

A Word from God on

Waiting

It's not a matter of doing; it's a matter of trusting.

I asked, "God, how do I get bold?"

God answered, "Worship and wait. Trust and believe. Believe that you will receive what you have prayed for; praise Me, for it is an act of faith. Watch and see."

> Not by might, nor by power, but by my Spirit, says the Lord of hosts.
> —Zechariah 4:6, ESV

God, what does waiting well look like for me?

Day 74

A Word from God on

The Vine

Come, and enjoy this day with Me. Joy is a fruit of the Spirit, so you can enjoy life irrespective of happenings and circumstances. I am your constant companion to guide you through whatever may come. Lean on Me. I am the Vine, supplying the nutrients to you, My branch, so you can bloom with the fragrant aroma of the gifts of the Spirit, drawing in others who could also use a breath of fresh air.

> I am the vine; you are the branches. If you remain in me and I in you, you will bear much fruit; apart from me you can do nothing. . . . If you remain in me and my words remain in you, ask whatever you wish, and it will be done for you. This is to my Father's glory, that you bear much fruit, showing yourselves to be my disciples. As the Father has loved me, so have I loved you. Now remain in my love.
>
> —John 15:5, 7–9

> For we are to God the pleasing aroma of Christ among those who are being saved and those who are perishing.
>
> —2 Corinthians 2:15

Your Six Minutes:
What Is God Saying to You Today?

Lord, show me how to fully embrace this day with You. How irresistible would that look to others who don't yet belong to the Vine?

Day 75

A Word from God on

The Faithful Gardener

With the right mix of nutrients, even a plant can grow right in the midst of a crack, but so can weeds. Plant the right seeds in every area of your life so the weeds are choked out and what is fruitful remains. Starve the flesh; feed the spirit. It's not about rules and regulations but simply inviting My Spirit in at every turn and asking, "What do I do here, now, in this situation, and that?" I will not mislead you, and your garden will surely flourish in My care. I tend, prune, and fertilize. I am a thoughtful, present, diligent gardener, and I love watching you grow.

But those that were sown on the good soil are the ones who hear the word and accept it and bear fruit, thirtyfold and sixtyfold and a hundredfold.
—Mark 4:20, ESV

So, what area in the landscape of my heart are we working on today, Lord? What needs extra tending, attention, care, sunlight, water, or pruning?

Day 76

A Word from God on

At Ease

The type of rest I give, you can have in the midst of work, strife, or battle: a soul rest, a soul at ease. You know who you are in Christ, and nothing can take that away. When you weigh the cares of this world up against that knowledge, you will always come out ahead. If you feel your foot is slipping, go back to this remembrance. Your position has nothing to do with you having it all together but instead, total dependence on Me because I have it all together. I hold you. Do as I say, speak as I direct, pray, and leave your cares in My capable hands. Remember, as I have helped and held you before, I will do it again. I know best. Rest and share this truth with the world.

> Come to me, all you who are weary and burdened, and I will give you rest.
> —Matthew 11:28

> When I thought, "My foot slips," your steadfast love, O LORD, held me up. When the cares of my heart are many, your consolations cheer my soul.
> —Psalm 94:18–19, ESV

Lord, is there an area where I've been striving and simply need to surrender to You? Speak to my heart, Lord. Let me soak in the truth of Your faithfulness throughout every season and situation.

Day 77

A Word from God on

Miracles

Continue to believe for miracles, for the impossible, no matter how long it takes. "If I can? All things are possible to him who believes" (Mark 9:23). Faith is the only prerequisite. Speak faith, speak life, and believe. Even if you're the only one. My people are a peculiar crew. I honor faith. Faith moves mountains as your faith aligns with My will (Matthew 17:20). My arm isn't twisted, but it's as if faith places your hand in Mine so you can walk with Me, in My way instead of your own. And trust Me, My way is full of amazing miracles. Think of the things the disciples witnessed when they walked with Me. Because they saw what I could do with the Father, they knew they could believe for the same, and even greater things shall they do!

> And Jesus said to him, "'If you can'! All things are possible for one who believes."
>
> —Mark 9:23, ESV

> Very truly I tell you, whoever believes in me will do the works I have been doing, and they will do even greater things than these, because I am going to the Father. And I will do whatever you ask in my name, so that the Father may be glorified in the Son. You may ask me for anything in my name, and I will do it.
>
> —John 14:12–14

Lord, no more sideline spectator faith. What do You want me to believe big for? Help my faith grow, as I believe You for the impossible.

A Word from God on

Hospitality

When preparing to welcome guests, the most important things you can give are a smile and a hug, opening your arms, your home, and your ears to hear even what remains unspoken. It doesn't matter if your home looks perfect. It's not about the things you share but how you make your guests feel. Where two or more are gathered in My name, I am in their midst (Matthew 18:20). Make it a party I'd want to attend. Be a Mary, not a Martha, and listen to Me through My people. Sit at My feet by engaging with My own. Don't do. Be. Be present; be open; be flexible; be engaging; be you. I've already equipped you. Trust that I've got you. I know how to have a good time. Remember that people are so much more than the small piece of them they bring during one encounter. They may come with their worst or best foot forward. Love them where they are, just as I love you in all your days and in all your moods, the full spectrum of you.

> Let brotherly love continue. Do not neglect to show hospitality to strangers, for thereby some have entertained angels unawares.
>
> —Hebrews 13:1–2, ESV

> "Martha, Martha," the Lord answered, "you are worried and upset about many things, but few things are needed—or indeed only one. Mary has chosen what is better, and it will not be taken away from her."
>
> —Luke 10:41–42

Lord, give me eyes to see people as You see them, and help me love them with Your love. What are You saying to me about this call to hospitality?

Day 79

The Power of His Love

Nothing in all creation can separate you from:

- My love
- My support
- My acceptance
- My help
- My guidance
- My guardianship
- My protection

I will finish what I started in You.

> Who shall separate us from the love of Christ? Shall tribulation, or distress, or persecution, or famine, or nakedness, or danger, or sword? As it is written, "For your sake we are being killed all the day long; we are regarded as sheep to be slaughtered." No, in all these things we are more than conquerors through him who loved us. For I am sure that neither death nor life, nor angels nor rulers, nor things present nor things to come, nor powers, nor height nor depth, nor anything else in all creation, will be able to separate us from the love of God in Christ Jesus our Lord.
>
> —Romans 8:35–39, ESV

God, what are You wanting to speak to me personally about Your faithful, dependable, never-ending love for me?

Day 80

A Word from God on

The Deluge

I speak in the fire. I am God over the messy, the deluge. I can handle it. I am the Lord. Is anything impossible for Me? Trust Me with the big and little things, and invite Me into all of it. I won't force Myself upon you, but when you give Me entrance into all areas of your life, watch Me move. I don't interrupt. I speak sometimes in thunder, but often in a still, small voice because I want your entire attention. Eyes on Me.

> The Lord sits enthroned over the flood [the deluge, the messy]; the Lord sits enthroned as king forever.
>
> —Psalm 29:10, esv

> And he said, Go forth, and stand upon the mount before the Lord. And, behold, the Lord passed by, and a great and strong wind rent the mountains, and brake in pieces the rocks before the Lord; but the Lord was not in the wind: and after the wind an earthquake; but the Lord was not in the earthquake: and after the earthquake a fire; but the Lord was not in the fire: and after the fire a still small voice.
>
> —1 Kings 19:11–12, kjv

> When the enemy shall come in like a flood, the Spirit of the Lord shall lift up a standard against him.
>
> —Isaiah 59:19, kjv

Lord, if there is any area I haven't surrendered over to You, show me and help me trust You enough to do so. I know You can make a miracle out of my messes if I give You access to them.

Day 81

A Word from God on

Becoming

When you consider others, see who they are becoming, not who they are now. I know the good plan I have for them; they have a hope and a future. It's blessed because I did the blessing. It's by My hand and not their own, so no man can boast; therefore, all can receive. There's enough to go around, and it's not dependent on them, or you, for that matter. If you simply reflect My love to them, they will flourish, their souls watered. I am the gardener, and I plant for growth. I weed and I prune too, and while it's not always pleasant, it's worth the end result.

> For I know the plans I have for you, declares the LORD, plans for welfare and not for evil, to give you a future and a hope.
>
> —Jeremiah 29:11, ESV

> For by grace you have been saved through faith. And this is not your own doing; it is the gift of God, not a result of works, so that no one may boast. For we are his workmanship, created in Christ Jesus for good works, which God prepared beforehand, that we should walk in them.
>
> —Ephesians 2:8–10, ESV

> For the LORD disciplines the one he loves, and chastises every son whom he receives.
>
> —Hebrews 12:6, ESV

God, is there someone You want me to see differently?

Day 82

A Word from God on

A Kingdom Perspective

A kingdom perspective is being able to look beyond the immediate circumstance or what someone says or does, and to the why behind it. The brokenness of people and the world causes people to make decisions without being completely informed or make inaccurate judgment calls.

Have grace for others, and find value in God alone.

> For our present troubles are small and won't last very long. Yet they produce for us a glory that vastly outweighs them and will last forever! So we don't look at the troubles we can see now; rather, we fix our gaze on things that cannot be seen. For the things we see now will soon be gone, but the things we cannot see will last forever.
> —2 Corinthians 4:17–18, ESV

> For the Kingdom of God is not a matter of what we eat or drink, but of living a life of goodness and peace and joy in the Holy Spirit. If you serve Christ with this attitude, you will please God, and others will approve of you, too.
> —Romans 14:17–20, NLT

God, is there something You want me to see differently?

Day 83

A Word from God on

Bold Love

Wherever you go, be My mouthpiece. Love people. Make love your highest aim. How can you love people without sharing My love with them? Be bold. You are bold in so many areas; it's time to get bold for the kingdom. Go about your day with intentionality. Stay in conversation with Me, and let Me guide what you say and do.

> But thank God! He has made us his captives and continues to lead us along in Christ's triumphal procession. Now he uses us to spread the knowledge of Christ everywhere, like a sweet perfume. Our lives are a Christ-like fragrance rising up to God. But this fragrance is perceived differently by those who are being saved and by those who are perishing. To those who are perishing, we are a dreadful smell of death and doom. But to those who are being saved, we are a life-giving perfume. And who is adequate for such a task as this?
>
> You see, we are not like the many hucksters who preach for personal profit. We preach the word of God with sincerity and with Christ's authority, knowing that God is watching us.

—2 Corinthians 2:14–17, NLT

*God, what does being bold in my ordinary, everyday life look like?
Show me what this means and how this translates for me.*

Day 84

A Word from God on

Working It

Spread My aroma in the workplace by showing your character. Be faithful, joyful, trustworthy, reliable, honest, hardworking, kind, gracious, forgiving, patient, and caring.

Radiate My love. Your colleagues need it.

> You are the light of the world. A city set on a hill cannot be hidden. Nor do people light a lamp and put it under a basket, but on a stand, and it gives light to all in the house. In the same way, let your light shine before others, so that they may see your good works and give glory to your Father who is in heaven.
>
> —Matthew 5:14–16, ESV

God, in what ways can I stand out for You?

A Word from God on

What You See

You don't see things fully the way God sees them. Do not jump and respond to your first instinct. Wait on the Lord. Sometimes I'll tell you to do something, and sometimes I'll tell you to be still and watch Me do it. Either way, I've got you, and I will see you through.

And he said to me, "What do you see?" . . .

And I said to the angel who talked with me, "What are these, my lord?" Then the angel who talked with me answered and said to me, "Do you not know what these are?" I said, "No, my lord." Then he said to me, "This is the word of the Lord to Zerubbabel: Not by might, nor by power, but by my Spirit, says the Lord of hosts. Who are you, O great mountain? Before Zerubbabel you shall become a plain. And he shall bring forward the top stone amid shouts of 'Grace, grace to it!'" . . .

"For whoever has despised the day of small things shall rejoice."
—Zechariah 4:2, 4–7, 10, ESV

For now we see in a mirror dimly, but then face to face. Now I know in part; then I shall know fully, even as I have been fully known.
—1 Corinthians 13:12, ESV

Lord, by Your grace, any mountain can be laid low. Help me admit I don't know it all and stay humble so I can see what You want to show me in every situation. Is there anything You want to speak to me about now? Anything You want to show me, something beyond the surface of what I can perceive in the natural?

A Word from God on

What Love Looks Like

What does love look like?

It is kind and understanding, seeing things from the other person's perspective.

It is patient, not forcing your own standards on someone else, and recognizing that each journey is unique.

It is long-suffering. I'm going to keep loving you no matter what, in what I say and do.

It keeps no record of wrongs; that only stifles growth.

> Love is patient, love is kind. It does not envy, it does not boast, it is not proud. It does not dishonor others, it is not self-seeking, it is not easily angered, it keeps no record of wrongs. Love does not delight in evil but rejoices with the truth. It always protects, always trusts, always hopes, always perseveres. Love never fails.
>
> —1 Corinthians 13:4–8

God, whose love tank can I help top off?

Day 87

A Word from God on

The God Factor

Don't forget the God factor. I'm in the midst of this. This is your chance to trust Me to be God.

> God is in the midst of her; she shall not be moved; God will help her when morning dawns.

—Psalm 46:5, ESV

Lord, where do I need to stop trying to do Your job and give You room to move?

Day 88

A Word from God on

Hearing Us

I love hearing from you. I delight in you. You are My treasure, and My Spirit dwells in you. My fire within you is like an eternal flame that never runs out of oil. The fire removes the impurities and provides light and warmth that attract others. It's that fire inside that truly attracts, not what's on the outside.

> The LORD your God is in your midst, a mighty one who will save; he will rejoice over you with gladness; he will quiet you by his love; he will exult over you with loud singing.
>
> —Zephaniah 3:17, ESV

> But you are a chosen people, a royal priesthood, a holy nation, God's special possession, that you may declare the praises of him who called you out of darkness into his wonderful light.
>
> —1 Peter 2:9

God, I ask You, please, for a greater revelation of the greatness of Your love for me.

Day 89

A Word from God on

Eyes on Me

Keep your eyes open. See with spiritual eyes what is placed before you, and remain alert and present in the present. Intentionally be intentional, purposeful, and deliberate, putting others' needs ahead of your own. Reflect My love by showing empathy for others. Do you, for Me. You are My vessel. Each one is unique; no two vessels look the same.

> I am the LORD; I have called you in righteousness; I will take you by the hand and keep you; I will give you as a covenant for the people, a light for the nations.
>
> —Isaiah 42:6, ESV

> If you keep yourself pure, you will be a special utensil for honorable use. Your life will be clean, and you will be ready for the Master to use you for every good work.
>
> —2 Timothy 2:21, NLT

Your Six Minutes:
What Is God Saying to You Today?

God, help me hear from You not just now but throughout my day, pausing to hear Your love notes, encouragement, guidance, and promptings. For now, help me hear what is on Your heart; share it with me as we begin the day's journey together.

Day 90

Pacesetting

Let Me set the pace. We run to obtain the prize, not aimlessly but with self-control and intention. Look at where you are going, and consider: Will it get you where you want to be? What's the destination? Are you headed that way?

> Do you not know that in a race all the runners run, but only one receives the prize? So run that you may obtain it. Every athlete exercises self-control in all things. They do it to receive a perishable wreath, but we an imperishable.
>
> —1 Corinthians 9:24–25, ESV

Lord, what is my calling? Where are You calling me to, or what are You calling me to do? Am I headed in the right direction, or is any course correction needed?

A Prayer of Salvation

If you have never surrendered your life to Jesus as Your Lord and Savior, you can pray this prayer to become a Christ follower today:

Lord God, I acknowledge that You are God, and I am a sinner in need of a Savior. I believe You sent Your Son, Jesus, to die on the cross for my sins and that He conquered sin and the grave when He rose from the dead. I receive Jesus as my Savior. Please cleanse me of my sins and come to dwell within me. Holy Spirit, fill me. I surrender my life to You today. Thank You, God, for the blood of Jesus that washes me clean! Thank You for a new life and fresh start, and thank You that I will spend eternity in heaven with You.

Yay! Read your Bible, find a great church to regularly attend, and tell people about your decision to follow Jesus and grow in relationship with God and the new family of believers you now belong to!

And everyone who calls on the name of the Lord will be saved.

—Acts 2:21

If you openly declare that Jesus is Lord and believe in your heart that God raised him from the dead, you will be saved. For it is by believing in your heart that you are made right with God, and it is by openly declaring your faith that you are saved.

—Romans 10:9–10, NLT

Everyone who acknowledges me publicly here on earth, I will also acknowledge before my Father in heaven.

—Matthew 10:32, NLT

Afterword

Dear Friend,

Congratulations on completing this 90-day journey. Truly pause for a moment and let that sink in. You showed up, day after day, choosing to quiet your heart and make room for God's voice. That is no small thing. In a world full of noise, distractions, and demands, you chose to listen. My prayer is that as you look back over these days, you can see that God has been faithful to meet you there, in the stillness, in the quiet, in the sacred space you intentionally made for Him.

As you close this book, my hope is not that you feel a sense of completion but rather that you feel a sense of commencement. My deepest desire is that this devotional would never be the finish line but the launching point of a lifelong habit of communing and conversing with your heavenly Father. Six minutes was never the goal; it was simply the doorway, a gracious, manageable invitation into a way of life marked by listening, partnership, and relationship with God through His Holy Spirit.

I also want you to know that I hope this isn't the end of our journey together either. It has been such an honor to walk alongside you through these pages, and I would love to continue to encourage you, learn with you, and grow together as we each pursue a deeper relationship with God.

If you'd like to stay connected, you can find me on Instagram, Facebook, and TikTok at @godminwithjulie. I'd love to continue this conversation with you there.

So don't stop now. Keep giving God the floor. Keep closing your trap (lovingly said, because I have to remind myself too 😊). Keep inviting Him off the couch and into the rest of your day. He delights in speaking to you, about the big things, the small things, and everything in between. May your prayer life continue to shift from monologue to conversation, from routine to relationship. And may you never forget, the God of the universe loves to meet with you.

With so much love and faith in what God will continue to do,

Julie

Notes